Some Alphabets

Opuntia is an imprint of Agincourt Press

Opuntia Books are published by
Luigi Ballerini
Beppe Cavatorta
Gianluca Rizzo
Federica Santini

Agincourt Press is a non-profit chaired by Berardo Paradiso

All manuscripts are subject to peer review.

All rights reserved.

ISBN: 978-1-946328-33-5

AGINCOURT PRESS
P.O. Box 1039
Cooper Station
New York, NY 10003
www.agincourtpress.org

© 2022 by Agincourt Press

John Latta

Some Alphabets

*With an Introduction
by*
Mark Scroggins

Agincourt Press
New York, 2022

for Joanne Kathryn Tangorra
and Giancarlo Louis Tangorra Latta
&
for Carmen *el doggo* (2002-2013)

Table of Contents

11	Marc Scroggins, *Diction, Form, Music: Latta's Letters*

I

19	Askance
20	Bent
21	Contempt
22	Doodle
23	Ennui
24	Flotsam
25	Gadabout
26	Hubbub
27	Indolence
28	Junk
29	Keep
30	Loathe
31	Muddle
32	Name
33	Offal
34	Poetry
35	Qualms
36	Rabble
37	Stuff
38	Tally
39	Umbrage
40	Void
41	Welter
42	Xerox
43	Yap
44	Zone

II

47	Amiable
48	Bluffing
49	Cordial
50	Daunting
51	Envoi
52	Folly
53	Gusto
54	Howdy
55	Innocent
56	Jongleur
57	Kid
58	Lowdown
59	Modern
60	Nod
61	Obvious
62	Palaver
63	Quiver
64	Rigorous
65	Shy
66	Truant
67	Usual
68	Vying
69	Wild
70	Xenolithic
71	You
72	Zero

III

75	Architecture and Mouth
76	Bracken and Porcupine
77	Camouflage and Naught
78	Dingle and Rack
79	Effigy and Oddity
80	Fragment and Vireo
81	Gangster and Wad
82	Hub and Buttercup

83	Idiot and Quagga
84	Jetty and Yellowlegs
85	Kingdom and Itch
86	Loudmouth and Zigzag
87	Marginalia and Aisle
88	Newel and Trim
89	Orthography and Fuck
90	Promontory and Clove
91	Quagmire and Jerk
92	Romp and Storm
93	Soot and Libido
94	Trumpet and Earwig
95	Umbrella and Knockabout
96	Vanity and Gash
97	Writ and Utterance
98	Xylophone and Dunce
99	Yammer and Xebec
100	Zephyr and Harness

IV

103	Animal
104	Bashful
105	Cuss
106	Diffuse
107	Emphatic
108	Feckthief
109	Gap
110	Homing
111	Idjit
112	Jaunty
113	Knob'd
114	Loud
115	Manner'd
116	No
117	One
118	Peopled
119	Quinine
120	Raw

121	Skinny
122	Toss'd
123	Upstirring
124	Volcanic
125	Whereas
126	Xylographic
127	Yak
128	Zoot

V

131	Ash and Mnemonic
132	Botch and Reticence
133	Cold and Arch
134	Dahlias and Stuff
135	End and Tool
136	Fracas and Quill
137	Gap and Erasure
138	Ha-ha and Cut
139	Integument and Pill
140	Jumble and Balm
141	Kudos and Xyster
142	Landskip and Fit
143	Master and Hazard
144	Need and Itch
145	Oar and Ytterbium
146	Plain and Unlikely
147	Quietist and Vitalist
148	Rasp and Duty
149	Slippery and Writ
150	Tumultuary and Nought
151	Uncial and Zip
152	Venom and Office
153	War and Jerk
154	Xenon and Kin
155	Yes and Gag
156	Ziggurat and Lurch

Diction, Form, Music: Latta's Letters

Form—the shape a poem takes—is evident, right there under our eyes or ringing in our ears: Augustan pentameter couplets, the blank verse of Elizabethan drama or Victorian epic, Burns's ballad meters and Swinburne's tumbling anapests; the skinny hesitancies of Robert Creeley's narrow stanzas, Charles Olson's sprawl, Susan Howe's jagged, overlaid fragments. *Content*, at a pinch, can be specified, paraphrased: Wordsworth describes his elation at a field of daffodils, Shakespeare laments impending old age (and not incidentally encourages a reluctant lover to take advantage of his ebbing passion), Dickinson imagines a genial carriage ride to the cemetery with Suitor Death.

A poetry's *diction*, however, is perhaps hardest of all to describe, to nail down; and it's in the gnarled wonders of its diction that John Latta's poetry has its most immediate charm. The 130 poems of *Some Alphabets* fizz between levels of diction—the demotic, the formal, the high theoretical, the archaic, the futuristic, the expansive, the pinched, the ordinary and the just plain *weird*—so that every sixteen-line stanza becomes a foray into the delightful unexpected.

Latta has always had a way with words, a kind of weighty insouciance everywhere evident in *Rubbing Torsos* and *Breeze*, his previous collections: the ability to spin out simultaneously concrete sensual observation, offhanded *bon mot*, and penetrating insight. *Some Alphabets* focuses that linguistic multi-tasking to an abbreviated, impacted pitch, and stirs into the mix a dark and glittering compost of sixteenth- and seventeenth-century language. Latta's years of work with the Early English Books Online project, digitizing and proofreading early modern texts, have given him a rich word-hoard to scatter throughout his own poems. "Stubbled profligate, I / Paw th'ancients, who paw me."

"The modern thing / To do now is languish / And fret about the self, / Its lit cigarette, its hunger—" Perhaps for some poets that is indeed the "thing." It's hard not to fret about the self sometimes, and Latta's poems indeed give us flashes of the personal Latta. But look what happens when he begins a funny conversation with his little son:

> 'I am the shy okapi'
>
> Is what I announce sillyly
>
> To my boy Giancarlo, five,
>
> Who winces 'na mare than
>
> A geaunte at the pincynge
>
> Of a waik man.' Talk
>
> Offers no 'corumpcioun,' is assuager
>
> To this 'sad and dyly-
>
> Gent pourveyance' the body.
>
> Variant renderings gauge what pluck
>
> Brings to charge audible meanders,
>
> Untangling cross flourishes, flytings, fables.
>
> We paint the earth with
>
> Wanton array, and thereto cling,
>
> Clay clot to clay. No
>
> Space do we not occupy.   ("Shy")

A tossed-off tongue-twister ("the shy okapi") is wrung through the "cross flourishes" of early modern diction till it becomes a comment on the body as "sad and dyly- / Gent pourveyance," on the "audible meanders…flytings, fables" of the language by which "We paint the earth with / Wanton array," and our own life on earth: stuck "Clay clot to clay."

What might not be immediately evident to the reader following the twists and tumbles of this effervescent language is the keen formal intelligence behind Latta's poems. They are, more than anything else, *musical* works:

Music's the main thing, bump'd

Up irregular, jawing, and clove

To angry like a pismire.   ("Promontory and Clove")

And music is not merely noise, but shaped, *formed* sound. I read the poems of *Some Alphabets* as formally inspired by the late work of one of the most musically-inclined of American poets, Louis Zukofsky (1904-1978). In the fourteenth poem of his collection *Anew*, Zukofsky quotes Plato's *Philebus*: "If number, measure and weighing / Be taken away from any art, / That which remains will not be much—" Early on, Zukofsky set himself to master the traditional forms and numbers of English poetry; in his later work, he experimented with new measures.

The Anglo-Saxon alliterative line counts stresses; English verse, since the Renaissance, has most often been accentual-syllabic, counting combinations of stressed and unstressed syllables:

That **time** of **year** thou **may'st** in **me** be**hold**... (iambic pentameter)
Be**cause** I **could** not **stop** for **Death**... (iambic tetrameter)

W. H. Auden, most famously, revived the stress-based line; Marianne Moore experimented with counting syllables without regard to stress. Zukofsky's late innovation, from the mid-1960s onward, is a poetic line that counts neither syllables nor stresses, but *words*. By the last-composed sections of his long "poem of a life" *"A"*, Zukofsky had settled on a five-word line; his final volume, *80 Flowers* (1978), contains eighty botanically-themed poems (and an epigraph), each of them consisting of ten five-word lines.

The poems of *80 Flowers* are impossibly dense constructions, black holes of quotation and transliteration in which syntax and reference have become occluded and indeterminate. Latta's alphabet poems, though they adopt the same five-word line, are more relaxed, jovial, humane. Their unit is that of sixteen lines—perhaps a doubling of Zukofsky's cramped count, or a nod to the sixteen-line "sonnets" of George Meredith's sequence *Modern Love*. The word-

and line-count is a guardrail, a boundary to keep the twitchy liveliness of Latta's language from spinning into an endless roller-coaster of surfeit. But the measure is more importantly a musical framework, a structure within which each poem takes its shape as a discrete etude, a sounding of the world.

Poetic form is never "natural," only a matter of accepted convention (convention, for instance, like the alphabetical ordering of the five sets of Latta's poems, each titled after a word or two plucked from its text). We cannot *hear* the music of the five-word line as we might hear Homer's hexameters or Pope's heroic couplets, but we can *see* the structure on the page, and as we read the poems, we realize how their structure has bestowed on them an angular music all their own. Form—ineluctable number, measure, and weighing—has channeled an infinitely varied diction into song.

I

Consider form as an imp

Position, a means to regulate

A hole wherein we see

Our deaden'd selves with a

Scribble of not-so-indifferent

Light in our eyes.   ("Knob'd)

Under one of its aspects, form may indeed be an "imposition"; but for Latta, it is a playful "imp" which allows the poet to awaken our "deaden'd" sensibilities, to scribble "not-so-indifferent" light across our eyes.

In "Yes and Gag" Latta posits his own work as a "hoyden'd counterblast to objectivist / Stringency" (Zukofsky, of course, was associated with the "Objectivist" poets). It is indeed that, I suppose; but Latta has taken the formal strictures of late Zukofsky and made of them a series of playgrounds and parterres of varied delights: "Go, book, attend the supple / Physical world, prise up the slop, / Finagle and romp…"

Mark Scroggins

Some Alphabets

I

I am hid.
—*William Blake*

ASKANCE

The notational omits the siege

Within with sumptuous digression regarding

Th'incapacity to map askance what

Tenacious marge we cannot do

Without. So we're off—Shanghai,

All motion still'd to inky

Lines, arcs and flysch troughs

Flying, or hiking the freshets

North to Onaway, Michigan, or

Sparr, economies of action reft

To probe th'attentive anywhere unprecedent'd:

High stoat region down to

Lumpish pink madrapore, and ungraspable.

I am not a Trobriander

Saddling up a palfrey mare.

I am no svelte pluck.

BENT

Aggressive, the formal ruses of

The sentence: that hodgepodge of

Sonic musketry in place of

Direct attack on the actual.

Artistic, the quashing of that

Action: in so doing we

Ignite the whole of N————,

Opening up a phase in.

With style opposing scale, movement's

Never content, but merely noise

For the composition: lumber lumbering

Off with duty split, armature

Unavow'd a grammatical feint unwoo'd.

Finally, a bomb follow up—

Evidence, put nicely, of the

Large bent the metaphysical is.

CONTEMPT

No jovial forestalling, no slender

Mephistopheles right down to throat-

Musculature, no coloratura bodybag... Monsieur

Monk, meliorist of scoff, accords:

'The motion between two lexicons

Is narrative.' Squads of putti

Fly banner'd by: 'something something

Th'impardonable cohesion of the new.'

Oh semantic champ, wolfhound devouring

Daffodil, all the slant inadequacy

Verbiage—like a witch—brooms

Up. 'Residual contempt *is* private

Significance, homeboy.' O sex me

Inexcludable into my fynisment, my

Throng, exemplum, you sans rien

That is not my fault.

DOODLE

Thank patience and Porlock, thank

The unclubbable leitmotiv, the glitch-

Made occidentalist hauling ass word

By itinerant word. Make that

Accidentalist. Considerable doodling betwixt there

Is: *très* big lexico-champs

Know how to make good.

Ordinary man hates the deafening

Dark, the spalling off of

Outer light until the within

Cries out for fusion or

Affect and nondeterministic programs call'd

Guarded commands go out making

Behavior mere mean to frequency

Of occurrence. *Right.* There're guidelines.

Somewhat unequal, more or less.

ENNUI

Post-biographical decoding of my

Pre-halcyon days, that's it.

Big nature grandstanding, and curtains.

Me and the kingfisher gone

Hoarse, rust-color'd, in bibs.

We finger the red clay

Tablets, condition *musée* brown-out.

Divvy up our impious scratches,

Boffins to technē and tactic.

We sail the Irrawaddy, astute

Stewards to a state of

Ennui too sinuous to gel

The floribunda, that word-happening

In daub-handy air. Another

Blueprint-explicit twosome, we drink

To post-lingual near-slaking.

FLOTSAM

Grand unwant'd bundles in dredgers,

Stuck in maws like ostentatious

Prayers intact, like bald zeros,

Like estuarine mortuary, befoul'd mayhem.

O like sidereal drubbings snott'd!

Flotsam you feasible you stride.

And a bare foot swings

Into view like a variant

Acquaintance or someone. Overlap in

The visual field a guarantee

Of increased apprehensiveness. Otherwise little

Of note happen'd, a narrative

Veil, oildrum, canister, a voluminous

Loop yanking against the concrete.

So we drift th'interface between

Phrasal and functional, optimal, moot.

GADABOUT

Too much a part of

Things to offer up too

Much, and coterie to thinking.

Behind a scrim of green

Leaves the museum of nothing

Is cornice and roof. Jitter-

Proof. String, invisible, knots up

Th'irresistibles of infectious want, that

Maison de passe in Honfleur,

Sun-slats combing the blue

Out of a sleeveless shirt.

To all flesh a reaching

Out that is normally pre-

Empt'd by pure intellect, empty.

Planks, the precise placing of.

Acquiesce, flub up, conduct, unspool.

HUBBUB

Arrest'd in lieu of to-

Do at end of day:

That diaspora involved with filmmaking.

Flaunting of the Arab burnoose

Increasingly view'd as incompatible culture-

Straddling, a ridge called Anthology.

It, unlike th'emergent, is task

Only to those who hold

To God's normal hubbub of

Routine empire: pointy and rubber,

Bras and girdles. Such constraints

Oft' doff'd as difference, that

Between a noun and a

Means of living. All that

Versus the history of science:

Texts untouched, or only peripherally.

INDOLENCE

A piety for it, con-

Firm'd habitué willing anon (*archaic,*

Immediately) to drink hobnob (Shakespearean)

Wif a bitty scullery maid

And scuttle off for coal-

Black Moxies anon (in one,

That is, later). There you

Have a case of it:

Th'indolence that mocks a perusal

(Attentive to detail) (skimming through

For any salient markers of

Use). Two definitions in skittery

Language it'd make one think

One 'must nat playe with

Hys sophemes and quyddities' as

The old copperplate's got it.

JUNK

Sailing the drug-skipper'd seven-

Zeroes—'mmm-mmm good.' Anguish

Of the scribal beast I

Got now trying to make

Ends meet means with reticent

Rain pinging away, that alphabet.

Every sentence 'a Sam Maverick

Branding not calf not Fence

Nor thicket,' junk the ticket

'Wif wch' to punch holes

In the phenomenal smear's untidy

Dispersal. The way language is

'One slipperier step or two

Away' gets drug up here

And 'luff' stretches—a goading

To sail nearer the wind.

KEEP

I 'keepe my self,' that

Is, withhold—skeptical, planetary, loud.

And suffer luminous intensity, cloud-

Wrought, fierce light hewn in

Amber air. Storm-pleat'd I

Be, aftermath to love's counterblast

Conceal'd. So the maple recalcitrant,

Unburdening. So the redbud kicking

Out the jams—'Green *is*,

Muh*fucker.*' In the 'donjon of

Mine owne selffe rude' I

Is apt erasure, hoodwinkery, privy-

Mimic to tempo gone quick,

To all that's bound up

In thee. Drear syntax and

Bed, its caustic, casual casuistry.

LOATHE

Common jazz quandary: Zoot loathe

To yield to Peabo, vague

Supernumerary to a hierarchy of

Lush greens in seasonal itch

For bramble and verbiage, fodder

To cake up galoshes and

Slicker, the better to bejesus

Heartache away, away. . . Oh blue

I am and posthumously famed

For th'inallowable rut of thinking.

I danger in the woodbine

With a critical topos going

Pop, bursting into the convolvulus

Like a mad hen, like

Any structural fulminant ready to

Waylay the piece, or not.

MUDDLE

An epitaph unwrit to dis-

Entangle the biographer's sorry scraps,

Her bare-ass'd sentimental Egypt.

Prof to a foray impractical

As it was influential, its

Degree of distortion an ether

Down out of the stars

To muddle the actions of

Men. All energy exert'd against

Any 'niggling conceptualism,' or any

Texte zur Kunst, and done

Up in an impeccably precise

Vocab. O for a rose

To hinder Silesius! Hers address'd

To a self in hiding,

Ominous exegesis, and unsimple hardware.

NAME

A veery is a thrush

With a note like its

Name yank'd thin enough to

Pull th'interstices of sun-up

Through it, that lattice of

'All lous language and lychtnes,'

Green havoc of spurge *a.k.a.*

Milkweed, whatever it is growing

There in amongst the tender

Burdocks that flange the nimble

Particular on verge of being

Counterfeit'd by address, or name.

It's a relational thing tangled

Up in nominalist array: noise-

Slurry engaging th'impure itch of

Material itself—bird, light, urge.

OFFAL

Is of no immediate use,

Is shiv'd off, is drag'd

Out, is 'durtie,' is 'suckt,'

Flung long and borne up

Again as scission and event,

The way the lingo itself

Is nothing: trotters and dross,

Chitterlings and scrap, a shaved-

Down rural poor nourriture, rich

Slag of it that is

Ongoing without. What thou namest

Will still not hat, not

Mussel, is offal to all

Continuing, gibberish reft of thing,

With a borrow'd washy outlandishness

That taketh the world off.

POETRY

It durst not merely gaze

In abandonment or plug up

The teleological with holes, uncountenanced

By anything beyond desire, new

Desire and its new science.

We get to its end

By beginning some other thing,

Shirtless and plugging away against

Whatever tall indifference moves in

To stake us to it,

The way any vaunt'd sign

Bringeth up a gall, or

Fool scarecrow drowning in fen-

Water, a poetry of such

Raucous subduing a Thracian ship

It is, and a venom.

QUALMS

Essence is just a quibble

With something or other, raw

Opprobrium for a trifling delinquency

Or pun, something to throw

A penny-heaven rife with

Earnests up against the yardstick

Of our appetite for naught.

To put a vogue rude

Noise to it: what I

Mean is the qualms you

Undergo—faint at the prick

Of consciousness—cut the quick

And 'tetch the Entiretie' of

The comprehended slot, there where

One's stuff is 'leaky Blab'

And one's word sweetly quare.

RABBLE

Spontaneity annex'd to hubris: soda

Prices merely a blip where

Use holes up inaccessible, blear'd.

Implicit in the quiddity is

Wind turbulent as rock, and

Other investigations announced as sun.

In the beshrunk word, coffer

To the damn'd, a thing's

Strident fermata's only one in

Allegiance to facticity's sour vertigo—

Fatti gravi: un solo modo

Per evitare il pericolo. Rabble

To tidy up the motherfucker.

Rabble oh boy, oh boy.

Looking like a scribble is

Not a note of ownership.

STUFF

I go poignant in mien

Like one lacking a fold,

All comfy outside the lofty,

Just another middling urban art-

Boy with a knack for

The arundinaceous particular. Oh hey

Now yourself. I did not

Come for any robust liaison.

I did not make metaphor

The stuff of a hookup,

Not *with* not *of* the

Almighty. I did not brook

Apology to th'effects of parallax,

My celestial body atomizing out

Into a fizz of coordinates:

Complicity one name for desire.

TALLY

Tenacious is the sex, yellow

Dwarf untiring, flame of my

Youth, ruin of a monk.

There's the slap and dehisce

Of wind-rankled signage, there's

The plain text lording it

Over two meagre daffodils. 'And

Under the blue welkin overarching

And grand, two cutouts, night-

Savvy, mimic the bustle of

Proscenium earth.' In nooks we

Turn to taunts, tout big

Our fraught yarns, divvy up

Our grim charms. The tally:

To trundle out a single

State's torsional, blinking, uncanvass'd loot.

UMBRAGE

Smack in midst of sun-

Stain'd badlands, a 'commodyous and

Plesant vmbrage' daubs down its

Shrewd badge, unpalatable, and against

Frank avowal. We who lie

Stirlessly wan succumb to 'all

The Bewtie of the fructuus

Feyld' the swapshop hideaway bed,

The pretense-mired commonweal, the

Shoe, the goat, the cheese.

Unrehearsed we be, and woe-

Pinch'd, moving to avoid th'immodest

And penetrant sun. Under cloud-

Happy umbrage, in green stench

Of shade undeliverable, words curtain

Off a mastery of things.

VOID

Bourgeois chic in the city

Occasions a joint erotic visibility:

Singly certifiable and avowedly hard.

To attack 'that old thing,

Art' by running it down

Is undoubtedly due: a simple

Nonverbal unreliability's just the thing—

Void avoidance, Zippo breakage, inestimable

Traffickings. Regions next any counter-

Factual attract, vaudeville to video.

Handheld mimetic preconditioning and all

Th'ardent orthographies of seeing, plus.

I a portrait in retreat,

One abrupt and publicly drawn

Out, genre melodrammatico, with all

Th'insolence, little gall, of th'autochthonous.

WELTER

At a massy distance, cloud-

Slabs, pumice-stones blotting up

A blue that defaceth memory.

So that: humble and Chaplinesque,

I soot lineaments of pathos

With grief 'like a foule

Bumbard' bee what doth droneth

With 'swiche glarynge eyen,' mad

Driveller of Saint Imbecile. Such

Is the welter-end of

Unmired fickle complacency—an obedience

Grim and unhistorical to language

And its laws. Here the

Paltry imitant sits, word-shorn

And insane, hewn and hand-

Scabbled, picking at its nits.

XEROX

A plangency in the thermal

Updrafts, and the oceanic body

All succulence and commingling, scooter

Tradewinds on the cha-cha

Boats and despondency: its fragrance

And accent covering it all.

Xerox is tumuli and barrows,

A dry continent, a surface,

And one's own unsheathed anticipatory

Soul mutter-stuck in tremolos

Of saying what utter'd oncet

Enters into heaven, *unh hunh.*

Oh that's how things were

In our mimeo-sniff days—

We dubious specimens, too, stencil-

Masters of our several selves.

YAP

Fat yap. I like speech.

I like how bowing here

In my buff'd-up Florsheims

Astraddle th'apparatchik welcome mat, I

Can say something pointlessly bogue

And have it drop forgettably

Into the air-coffers: *plink.*

'Yo, threshold' I say, or

'Abrode to wend, to take

The ayre' or some heterochthonous

Garrulity that queers a smash

Mouth. I like the rhythms

Of speech. Like the tizzy

Of a cloudlet of feeble-

Wing'd gnats thronging in squadron

To salute my big ears!

ZONE

That final lassitude. Oh shepherdess.

Fed up with Greek antiquity,

Drowsy and remiss. The ample

Sky fills up with thousands

Of soot-daub'd swifts circumnavigating

Fiery smokestacks. 'To God, to

God' the chittering goes: hungry

Men bang incinerators open one

By one. 'What falshede is

In mariage' means the sign

Is hanging off the door.

So the dare, the haughty

Zone, th'unpresuming shrug. So th'immense

Defiant pity for what one

Cannot say. Moon is not

Moon, moon is sawn bone.

II

Wisdam forsothe is drawen of hidde thingis;
ne ther shal be maad euene to it topasie of Ethiope,
ne to the most clene steynyng shal be comparisound.
Job XXVIII, 19

AMIABLE

Twenty or so hawks dot

A thermal updraft, and kettle—

Movement or action is 'home'—

And faith is a sort

Of ferment, something to wring

Out a soul-dry tenacity,

Or mettle. Grand amiable in

The continual onslaught of fictive

And mistake, I let residual

'Myldnesse' record the caught superfluity

Of my digs. Suitcase up-ended

In bathtub, key under rug-

By shirt cover'd with land-

'Scapes i' the imminent deadly

Breach' of what mumble th'insane

Lexicographers of 'Bedlam' to 'Bethlehem.'

BLUFFING

Not the restless parry of

Cars blistering the turnpike, not

Talk beginning to pale—admits

To us the violent thrall

Of what we come to

Like. We flourish under stern

Adult looks on perfect stretches

Of fog-demur yard. We

Do sketches of toy animals

In revolt, the odd apothecary

Jar, things 'put down &

Next expunct'd' and a crowd

Of fowls. Bluffing gets us

Into rooms we never thought

We'd see, neglect of history,

Scale, 'the peril it bring.'

CORDIAL

The new damask cloth is

Spotted with someone else's slinging

A cordial, noisette. Grownups do

Nothing—bicker with slow-dying

Friends, & get potted. Today

Is getting late for bicycling

The road parallel the new-

Mowed fields kept up by

The state. Under a dusk-

Sized coverage of gloom we

Nudge our fallible bodies up

To bed, admired for what

Antics precede a sonic boom.

The rouge-fiery stars'll oversee

The night, the forsythia'll hike

Up its fame-yellow'd skirts.

DAUNTING

A daunting map is all

We got, smudgy-ink'd in

Green relief. It lends airs

Of disbelief to our fever'd

Marginal lot. Books we read

Are the sort antiquarians recommend—

The frenzy of a zealot's

End, the history of a social

Obligation, sexual exercise for sport.

Out the tent-flap door

One sees the piercing blued

Stretch of a lake obtrude.

An envoi reports 'the way

Is mere wavering,' unmark'd, and

Apt to sully souls used

To hours of senseless hammering.

ENVOI

'A scent of shallots lathering

Up,' is a mean sign-

Forged trivialization of the real—

'Shallot' a class-marker, maketh

A kind of vocabulary congeal

Rich, or attests to no

Sup beyond one's just squeaking

Through. So the prodigal wavering

Ensues, a well-machined axis

Of syntax and sham 'to

Spellenn to the follc summwhatt'

That that an envoi do.

'Go, book, attend the supple

Physical world, prise up the slop,

Finagle and romp, or drop

The word-borne thing, uncouple.'

FOLLY

The glorious fit of I

With self now unsprocket'd is,

Disjoint, and lame. A bicycle

Tips its rider into flame-

Yellow leaves, grim and weedy

Pelf. Constancy is no sweet

Drama; no tumble or provender's

Got by folly, lounging smitten

Against some unadornable door for

Some fast soldier's comic snort.

Self a constant derelict is,

Vagrant to 'thy mien, thy

Tones, thy motion.' Inactivity is

No stageable beast. Without act

Nothing's apparent. Just bicycle prop'd

Against tent, and rider deceased.

GUSTO

Uncertain of the rules, lash'd

By disarming inexactitude, no husbanded

Play, meager, nude, now resurrects

What's nigh on quash'd. Th'ongoing

Animal delight in marshaling a

Trove of love-manoeuvres secure

Admits gusto as mere human

Toxic imbalance, or blight. So

The usual spring abounds, trawling

A too delicate sun across

Lawns where rude boys run

And choose up sides with

Aimless sounds. And words 'withoute

Oony withholdyng' make public rut

With a fayre 'what if'

And all evidence kaput forthwith.

HOWDY

Oh the poignancy of men

Pouting, fisticuffs in the offing.

A kitten scoots off: wild

High-ass book. In solitary

Breach talks the mouth 'Howdy'—

Inconstant, beatific, remote. I is

A disarming, a commonplace, dogging

The geek suburbs, its compliance

To terror come up under

Initiative, self stuck in cosmogonic

Chorus juggling conjunctions like 'and.'

Fields of weather dump down

Rain, flux and hint a

Smeary articulation, poppy and Saint

John's wort. Integrity is cued:

Halt and nod and go.

INNOCENT

'Bifel that in that sesoun'—

Two-ply beginning to what

A residuum of lines unties.

Thus innocent fate redounds consequence

To itself unforeseen, and makes

Time a nigh-visible thing.

A gibbon, toy, is prop'd

Up next to a couch

Unavailing and randomly lit. Out-

Doors a cardinal booms out

A brusque 'what cheer' like

A gush or veil of

Blood or a boy saying

Something that sounds like 'ouch.'

Volatile market, season of beasts—

'Goo to thy sopper sadly.'

JONGLEUR

Hullydum optimum scorch to 'erre

And pupplische a sentence contrarie,'

Oh Jongleur of the Nail!

You spot an inhabitable moment,

English it into the world—

Two caribou thrill to sky-

Vault thirls and pause hoof-

Trepid in alarming occidental light.

Lichens stubble the hemispheric monument.

Bird-splash rakes the screed

Incised there, impenetrable list of

Pardonable deeds. Caught: one minimum

Incontestable rent in th'unexpressive he-

Stitchery of the ongoing song:

'Werrse & werrse drinnchess, &

Att te lattste drunncnenn be.'

KID

Pixiness in the sun-rubble,

Gangsters chucking champ goods all

Through Elysium neighborhoods, debits enter'd

In a column mark'd 'plausible

Trouble.' The consequence of genre

Is furniture. One way of

Maintaining dignity in stark arousal.

One way of seeing how

Measure under duress is insistence,

An unmistakable bulge. Going downtown

To scoop up something 'rustical,

Too pointless for the city'

Or acting like a kid

With a sandwich-end teetering

Between two fingers, or half-

Way up to a mouth.

LOWDOWN

Preempting a call to 'camp

It up' in high acreages

Of flesh, such motion ratifies

Mutual rash impermanence, like 'hiccup.'

Parity is achieved, that party

Plank, by precise placement of

Frank audibles in interleaf'd acoustic

Puzzles. 'And by ese, soffte—

Clymben tyl thow kome aloffte.'

The lowdown districts acquiesce, plummeting

Realigns the soul. The body's

Imprecise contours console whatever gods

See unfit to bless. Dirty

Noise subsides and dolor does

Its work in human dark,

Reach and here-dapple deny'd.

MODERN

The morning drizzle kept up

Through noon, voluble by turns.

One commentator got voted 'most

Undetermined.' I don't get it—

The world. The modern thing

To do now is languish

And fret about the self,

Its lit cigarette, its hunger—

Variance exposed by turn or

Temper atrudge behind a plow.

Strong zonal westerlies bring in

A dumbshow of clouds, all

Banking on lively crowds of

Tantric warp and bunko artist—

The name is 'wyl feynt

To be nyce and queynte.'

NOD

Each raindrop pursues its one

Fell intent to make its

Way into the absent visual

Field that becomes a lake

By adding blue, a pigment.

Here a human nod *is*

A universe. It tumbles out-

Lying cogs into gear, takes

The 'tenement that Walter Mydnyght

Sometyme held in the parissche

Of Gales' and deposits it

'Bitwene the lond of Raaf

Sturdy' and the telos that

Is feed to any sentence,

Is its evidence, pooling up:

'& is with-owte date.'

OBVIOUS

Of course. Stupid of me.

Hunkering down near the kohlrabi,

Scrounging around for anything new,

Partial humidity with clearing rains,

Lightning ascent in acting 'clubby.'

Yesteryear's fucks come back: arcane

Torsos mount'd with spiritual spit.

The absence of everyday life

Is obvious. You muff'd it.

Insane. Typically a big leap

To avoid unpleasant scenes—compendia

Of teen wit in talk,

Mannerist and undeter'd, of creeps.

And me likewise acquires that

Tittery Proustian mystery, uncertain escapades

In ruins I sincerely doubt.

PALAVER

'Pon arrival territorial, two otters

Lick'd Saint Cuthbert all up

And down, what he 'gaf,

Grauntyd & confirmyd by his

Wrytynge.' He a gamy wiseacre

Even in a massacre, he

A faunalist amidst the tumulus

And knell of a confuzioun,

Brain blocage and reeling. 'Sum

Wold play & sum sayd

Naye.' So a summer begun,

& welcome, image of impermanence,

Solicitor against the doom of

Reason resounding, goon on pilgrimage—

He do page against page

In lieu of a camouflage.

QUIVER

Tiny hammocks of moisture adhere

To coppery pipes, lighting up

A laundress's plaids and stripes,

Or plunging into linen's boisterous

White vibrato. An impudent shirt-

Factory boss, rudeness in rut-

Regalia, assails the pink financial

Page like a stench. Quiver

Of yesses in the image-

Cloister! Tedium gone unto cloud-

Mischief—'harm vnto jape'—where

A solitary canoeist J-strokes

Into a wake. Superimposed, partial,

He's made music in th'indices

Of a thing, there where

Th'exit irrevocable must present itself.

RIGOROUS

Gibberish in the rigging monkeys

Up the signal the way

The blub of sentiment fouls

Up candor to cream receipt.

Yeah. We lather to define.

We dross the radiophonic word,

Scat the pure invect. 'All

Volatils of the eir maaken

Nestis in swiche nestis' is—

What the goons rigorous drub

Us with—pure static of

Discrepancy unmarred. It is not

Wisdom impudent and criminal. It

Is 'drawen of hidde Thingis,'

And 'euene aftir most clene

Steynyng shal not be comparisound.'

SHY

'I am the shy okapi'

Is what I announce sillyly

To my boy Giancarlo, five,

Who winces 'na mare than

A geaunte at the pincynge

Of a waik man.' Talk

Offers no 'corumpcioun,' is assuager

To this 'sad and dyly-

Gent pourveyance' the body.

Variant renderings gauge what pluck

Brings to charge audible meanders,

Untangling cross flourishes, flytings, fables.

We paint the earth with

Wanton array, and thereto cling,

Clay clot to clay. No

Space do we not occupy.

TRUANT

Becalming is the pericarp, its

Pale red lucre of enclosure,

Only color residing within, sure

The way air is sure.

Truant too, perilous for us

Mock uprights, spathes unsprung. A

Pond is like that: algal

Bloom hung to sag-edge

Under fire-dents made by

Sun. In my innocent sweat-

Weather, I am a cloud

On stilts, cloud Vlad th'Ineffable,

Moist, leggy, churning: 'O mysrewly

Lyfe I wyl be stedfast

As any stone. Crabbidly seid,

And schrewdly for the nones.'

USUAL

In usual dudgeon regarding my

Dagger hilt, and how asinine

The lake is, its squib

Of a sunset. Therein 'to

The crimson swatch' I enter,

And, yours in skank rectitude,

Do 'enter into a palsy.'

Oh to feign without faith

Is fabulous mire. See. Such

Lies *like* the occasional falsehood—

Something tin-ear'd and abrupt.

Rogue constraint to offer up

The difference between indifference and

Unlatch'd nounal inpropinquity, that desire

To scope out anything discrete

Hamper'd by the paroxysmal come.

VYING

The 'revolting crudity' of my

Misspent youth is something of

A ruse and misnomer, all

Of it a bookish rehash

Of Homer—a vying, taciturn,

Sentimental, uncouth. Just as all

Stamina is benign and aesthetic,

The hapless mired insufficiency of

A particular crew gone loony

In the night-blue vestibule

Of ocean, turning down lamps

Under which lies the last

Good map. O clockwork God,

Sit teetering on a fulcrum—

'The sunne is maad blak,

As a sak of heire.'

WILD

Another slavish munificence is built.

And gentle souls do roar.

Into a wild season that

Bored out a radical negligence

As one way in, sweeping

Piety and guilt *both* along

In holy ambush. O God,

Pricketh thy last envelope of

Heaven, let sigh one thousand

Sighs in mad irredeemable *retour.*

You know the type, used

To getting the obligatory structures

Built: stove-in arks, dumb'd

Down blobs on stilts. Disencumbrancer,

'Laat thyngges that mowe nat

Been be, & bee stille.'

XENOLITHIC

Scrambling down a northern field,

South-tilt'd, gravelly, plow'd, I

Found, heart-shaped, a jasper—

Stone the color of dry

Blood embedded in a yield

Of basalt. Uplandish it is,

And strange, thus to tame

The brutal commonweal of rock

By game rote grammars, and

Flange. Anything, rib or rim,

To surround the uncult invect

And raise the xenolithic welt.

Somewhere some fair field unheeded

Lies fenceless, unlanguaged and untask'd—

'Hiss drinnch wass waterr,' it'll

Say, 'hiss Mete wilde rotess.'

YOU

Limn no attempt to lob

A euphoric yes again against

The 'verray trowthe syk &

Languysshynge,' that fob design intact

On refuse piles. One loathe

To stymie such private toys

As these belies the Edenic

Ease of chatter robust. A

Noise in the conference hall

Brooks both the investigatory whatnot

Of insane selection (fat-witted

In the faubourg) and the

Snottiness of choice (frank nullities

In the spy code thereabouts).

You begin to have doubts—

Muscular, foul-hearted, particular, rank.

ZERO

Nothing is what is not

Something, or a capacious big

Bag of the ineffable minus

Zero, brief largesse and laud,

What the departmental prick offers

Up to leverage a supremacy,

Affable, withholding. Nothing is plea-

Bargain against pleasure—'all flowre

Of maidennes she shal bee /

Of Maidyns All she shall

Be flowere,' all totemic pointillism

And quondam half-ass get

Out. Dying never enter'd in.

I quit the bobolink up-

Rising and falling in meadows—

Nothing will get me back.

III

> ... the lid there's a sounding-board; and what
> in all things makes the sounding-board is this—
> there's naught beneath.
> —*Herman Melville*

ARCHITECTURE AND MOUTH

Carnal bridges offer one out,

A satisfying architecture, humping up

To the prospect, semi-wild,

Of looking down. Green stalks

Green to recoup continual greening,

Stalks a fat weed-wrack'd

Mouth to burble out dark

Arpeggios of gaping predatory loss.

Loss that eats loss—sex-

Slung feasibles of hungry intent.

So sound errs to lend

Repetition its holy score: I

Rinse myself of any too-

Godly freight, and fail to

Hush my own heart's blood

That down unbent flowers flows.

BRACKEN AND PORCUPINE

Brute debut: blood lust bounding

Out midnight against sneezy waddle,

And salt-crave. Of bracken

Made is memory and its

Smell, a rope pull'd taut

Enough to hum into diminishment

At merest tremor. A porcupine

Incisors creosote off the cabin

Porch. My father shotguns it.

In a mediaeval village it

Is raining blood, the meconium-

Drip and offal of thousands

Of newly-Emerg'd Paint'd Lady

Butterflies. There along the Temple's

Whited Wall, Phlegmatick lazy Dreams,

And not wing'd at all.

CAMOUFLAGE AND NAUGHT

That anthem of lonely grief

And stout shoes clambers up

Music's back, back up into

The feverish stars. The black

Robe of night inadvertent and

Arousing, unsuitable object for mirth.

My consciousness is a burin

Routing out a shallow canal

Where the floody body goes

Recumbent, jejune. A prig camouflage

For pretense, or a gag.

Lying is a stock concocting:

Billiard ball lasso'd by noose,

Atmospherics 'took' by voice vote.

In the languishing is naught,

A speedy mutable viability caught.

DINGLE AND RACK

Oh th'inconstant rub of newsy

Sequentiae: that the dingle is

Toss'd abysmal, floody, and we—

Idle-pated by rancor—adrift.

That on the seaswept shingle's

Dun, quacks in love do

Horseplay, bereft of fun. That

All the glib-quick ranks

Deliverable diploma'd do get, hair

And rack. That men's loves

Are but afflictions. That titles

Raffle off and still ambition.

That to bee a King

Be Fame's butte. That news

'How paucitous be it' torqued

Is stay against th'inebriant dark.

EFFIGY AND ODDITY

Sunk. A plectrum to plunk

Against th'impenetrable plenitude, to torture

Out the 'dreegs and chaffes' of

Fable and doctrine, effigy of

Song. And so exhorteth He

We to good workes continval

Mortifying flesshe. 'Men love

Me with there lyppes and

There heartes bee farre off

Me.' Prayer and mumblings of

Oddity: to lavish slavish attention

On a towardly and pregnant

Soil, the heroic thing is

To persevere in stupid stupidly.

An historic eros is come.

A droplet is pending off.

FRAGMENT AND VIREO

A century and a half

Of vapid commentary mere tinkering

Only corroborates: naked model still

Muddy blue looming against red

Earthwork of ravine. Any fragment

Is proof: arbitrary, luminous and

Unique: an heretofore uneasy marriage.

That is a statement, and

Fecund, and no logic abides

Th'unruly erotic, torn by language

Devoid th'actual wrapped and quick

Narcotic. One raw gaze assembles

The real surround just as

Whosoever dares love untiringly sleuths

And figures: vireo a burr

In th'adamant wash of sound.

GANGSTER AND WAD

Chance is rampant here, even

Adjusting for the pale gangster

Complacency of usual hagiographic burn,

Whatever that be. Manoeuverability's th'essential

Modernist harness—or my name's

Not John Partial. And I

Ain't squatting here reading 'Homey—

Don't you play with dat'

Cut into the stall with

A needle. Big sun out

There drilling the tree-toss'd

Yard. To name a thing's

A double grope: rind of

Orange tumbling into a wad

Of towels. Stubbled profligate, I

Paw th'ancients, who paw me.

HUB AND BUTTERCUP

Out of the granular fog

A God-mad and petulant

Orison to dispel all doubt:

Hub of things mortal. Stag

Cached in hazelwood, codpiece aslant

In a meadow of rue

And salsify. Something black-legged

In pursuit of the green

Aphid in the center of

That buttercup is teetering, tentative

Following the miscue language is

Unaware of without the pressure

Of a creed for unsaying

It. Stray companions of our

Misapprehension: pushing nose into flower

To muster-nub the burgeon.

IDIOT AND QUAGGA

Idiot say he going t'accessorize

'S style with story: —*oh*

Rain, ye bellwether of my

Sulk. Jetting in Histrionickal pride

I saw how Measure doth

Exemplifie the Harty dome, so

As to Swage and Modefye.

'What lacketh measure is none

Aduauntage.' The fuzzy, and

Furry, distinct is thus: one

Mire of the credible. Yonder

Sulphur butterfly is doing complex

Stitchery in bog-foetid air.

—The private stuff'd sphagnous moss

Into a hole, gunshot-sized,

Color of Charles Fourier's quagga.

JETTY AND YELLOWLEGS

Stellar brooding in the brine-

Lanes. World call'd 'a Bote,

Toss'd it is, over &

Onto' troublous nethery foregone waves.

Dogging the jetty it is.

Devotee of the trawler-dump,

Cur of the opalescent trough

Askitter. Up-down amongst fisher-

Folk, a dean of disjumble.

Oh the doubleness does sur-

Round us & meeter be

It to name than to

Abide the doughty spits of

Cloudwork ravishing th'ecliptic where two

Lesser yellowlegs lift off two-

Noted, he sd, *you, you.*

KINGDOM AND ITCH

I love the faintly illicit

Nights of memo and draft,

Supper-in-a-box deft-

Cook'd in its lyrical cardboard.

The fetch of sleep quick-

Claims my boy member of

Its kingdom the color of

Oil the color of lemons.

One grows indomitable under comical

Light, longs to parse fables

Of paterfamilias and strop, rye

And brute melancholy. 'O pig-

Headed darling of my autumnal

Frenzy, return with that alarming

Booty, I itch terribly and

Irregular, frog on bent knee.'

LOUDMOUTH AND ZIGZAG

A terror made me gentle

In that scorn hemmed-in

Prefecture, and lapse and rebuttal

Made me ace my quarrel-

Some years, just another loudmouth

Under-laurel'd. Say *I am*

Not the one who boo'd

The universe, and you ain't.

Saint Venial of the Texts—

Here a crow hangs aerial

And inconsequent like a tilde.

Against most devout ejaculation, mere

Nuzzling, humblest zigzag of earth.

Against incontinent human Frailtie cruel,

Extreamst madnesse natures up first

Error, and consum'st our daies.

MARGINALIA AND AISLE

My marginalia's sentimental and fey,

Gypsy-spelt, and dagger'd to

Improbable rows of ibids, exclamatory,

Amateur, scorn'd. Addressed to you

Out there, fiddler and deft

Almanacker of the elegiac gone.

Oh the ache and sustenance

Of ache, what makes th'hearty

Soprano's satin'd nipples stiffen up

To buttons mid-aria, admitting

The clamor and succor of

Lack. It's lack th'octagonal stick

Of the mad-saw'd violin

Hides, a pernambuco beaut' with

Silver-mount'd ebony frog, avowedly

Invisible here in the aisle.

NEWEL AND TRIM

Pieces filch'd here and there

In minor conjunct. Style frees

Itself of the function of

Padding out knowledge or story

And destiny's refusal is another

Is, what refusal's answer 'doth

Furder.' No more unbegown'd Zeno,

Detoqued and ready to unlace

Philosophy. No more Sundaying over

Sunday with Sunday. I fain

Dance the hay in pixilated

Light, a philodendron leaf twining

Unsheath'd up the newel post

In loyal consort to some

Tuneful mighty fret of weather—

Vatic, delinquent, suant, and trim.

ORTHOGRAPHY AND FUCK

—Ah put a spell onch

Chew. One kind of orthography

To fetch up a milieu.

Spelling is 'data rich,' subtle

The way sex is, venting

Substance into the void fervid,

A way to get it,

The act, going. Spelling out

Makes susceptive th'exemplary ex nihilo,

A most welcome moisture, lather.

Short period of reaching for

Things with nimble hands, unsuitable

Objects of mirth. Dimensions of

A letter lugged, an F

With which to begin it:

Fuck and untried vasty possibles.

PROMONTORY AND CLOVE

Music's the main thing, bump'd

Up irregular, jawing, and clove

To angry like a pismire.

Or like camphor spill'd ajostle

Vett'd by vague local breezes

The way a promontory slaps

Th'oceanic surround. Oh enough hand-

Wringing eloquence about the under-

Story dwarfs. Near the bowling

Green a pinch'd laugh impinges:

Clarity's a twit. City night-

Clubbers off work pitch butts

At cab-stirr'd light yellowing

With possibility, and sill plants

Lash out at the three-

Dimensional air, attempting to leaf.

QUAGMIRE AND JERK

'Rule thy toong, I would

Thy Clappe weare shut vp.'

In yonder parsnip field by

The truck farm a lyric

Jerk is doing pratfalls in

A swank profusion of hepatica.

He's a jusqu'auboutist. He's happiest

In a quagmire of copulae:

'And one sunny day Tom'

Is how the boy's story

Beginneth: haboundance with figure solitary,

Slash and prattle of sun-

Spasm against the dogged cloudworks,

And figg for the critickall

Indices, stuck in the Lump

And Loynes of it all.

ROMP AND STORM

Radiance crosses a room like

A fever-canister, brief salvo,

Desire's name caught without rescue

Above boy-romp and traffic.

Out in the thrashing sun-

Light I see how nightshade

Hauls itself up the storm

Fence like a convict, jangles

Its deadly little flowers. It

Isn't love makes me thus

Connect, we hoist and carry

All that for what we

Got no name. Chigger-brash

The sorrel's weedy obligados thrive

In sun where you are

Nameless and I am coming.

SOOT AND LIBIDO

Loan'd out airs 'dunna' diminish

Thee, spunk-rev'd reversal of

Line's own libido. 'I turn

To taunt's soot and yarns, / I

Fake a modern folly / And

Knuckle down among schoolmarms / Who

Snicker at my dolly.' In

A brain the size of

My diminishing red pencil lead

The rufous hummingbird 'holds' charts

Of nearly ten thousand trumpet-

Flowers dispersed over dozens of

Locations, 'nectar'd' and 'de-nectar'd'

Kept infallibly distinct. A stuck

Tractor spews clods of dirt,

Spume shaped like a sneeze.

TRUMPET AND EARWIG

In a woods near Ermenonville

I sliced into a trumpet-

Brassy peach and ate it

Unconcernedly slouch'd against a black

Gangster car. A couple nigh

In rut: two earwigs skitter'd

Under a stone. So tempo

Is the raggedest tender, up-

Scorch of a kind of

Discursive barn-burning, or hand-

Raising, much of it verily

Fictive, though its nouns are

Correct, *sauf* Ermenonville, as is

Proper. So 'Love in tonge

Cann'st last longe,' the taut

Word is a rotten cord.

UMBRELLA AND KNOCKABOUT

Let the mornefull Cipresse dy,

It is umbrella to us,

Soft-voiced, like a tsar.

Or a member grown big

In a kind of plight

To do its end. Legacy

Again more convivial than plunder'd,

Like the urban endive, like

He who sitteth happy on

Apollo's knee, that cunny kisser!

Old arrogance of origins in

God-tangle, writing a conspicuous

Impudence and vendetta to rhythm,

Scuttling crab-legged into each

Knockabout world without idol, God-

Solace nigh, like a wasp.

VANITY AND GASH

Doodads and rickrack lounge about

The vanity, oh the short

Shelf-life of fashion! its

Tawdry links—accessory, comestible, trot!

Repartees of angle and sash,

Nickerings before mirrors when what

We cats need is scat-

Moan busting up the cubist

Firelight. I got ricochet and

Hinge, gash and rabble against

The departmental score. I done

Made my mental tally. I

Got rain sharpening its claws

Up the rooftop. I do

Lope through the assailant damp.

The tub sits denudedly white.

WRIT AND UTTERANCE

Goeth rumor by kopje and

Semaphore: a feral seer cometh.

I doubt it not. It

Ravels with the writ and

Globe of my seeing, meat

Of the grass-limned conjunction-

Less veldt. I jimmy open

Shackles of utterance with a

Pencil the color of thin

And feckless, a stagey scrawl

Where haze writes up horizon.

Haul up the stays, oh

My reck and corazón. My

Glance'll probe and lance any

Landscape of th'unspoken, where nothing's

Ease is my singular coitus.

XYLOPHONE AND DUNCE

Turn a rub-color'd eye,

'Such a waggish leering it

Works in all your horribles.'

Nigh is th'impenetrable buckler of

'Insolency Rote and snarlish,' wrought

Butt of cheer-raked quarrel,

In 'formall noddy' to puffery

Careerist. Oh the drear of

My dissemblance bangs a murtherous

Xylophone, 'theen I besseche thee.'

You in the baffle-hat

And plush fatigues, tired of

Pulling th'impartial rabbit out, that

Nutmeg-ear'd one. Blake Wm,

'I am hid,' dunce of

Bliss unsung, idiot of rose.

YAMMER AND XEBEC

Sere neologisms of sleep, a

Yammer of tensiles, cataract of

Like and like: intolerable rubbishes.

That's the kind of thing

Gets a boy hardy, or

Spavined and juvenating into one

Of two dirty socks. 'Away

With All Learning & Immodesty,

The very Grammar is prophane,

Instructs in th'obsenenesse of Conjunctives

Copulatif, and what a smell

Thinke you are the likes?'

Xebec abangled in stars, Lord

High Regent of the distraught

Night & all to do

With 'bokis of ornat enditynge.'

ZEPHYR AND HARNESS

There. We cry our flurry'd

Adornment against the big T,

And its unremitting thievery. Here—

A zephyr in a harness.

Prod and stowaway, maddish with

Motive, its grace a raw

Advert to green youth, apparel'd

In light. Here's the place

To say in good sadnesse:

My solid Johnson made muse

Of a Cocke, after such

Joyning of giblets joylesse. Common,

Sayeth, as the barking of

Dogges. And thou shalt be

Stellified and big, hombre, say

I, with my peremptory sass.

IV

Alas, the solid pencil itself
as fingered briefly by Hugh Person
still somehow eludes us!
—*Vladimir Nabokov*

ANIMAL

Animal, erring, and indomitable, you

Seethe and squinch as I

Yoketh thy eye in eyes

'That can do hurt,' a

Force the eye cannot be

A part of, the scenery.

Against numbingness, my bottomy days

Of black ink and urine-

Hued forsythia'll have ruined your

Proofs futile, feasible as the

Love-dalliance of a ferret.

That one eye starest into

Its geminal other in cold

Tardy putter and minuscule fub,

Intellectually resilient as rump telegony,

Corporeally incipient as a blush.

BASHFUL

Bashful, lyric and monumental, I

Horse around, hymning these joyous

Plangencies wörtlich, thankful for simple

Refrains. "—*Go, book, go, thine*

Annals of an Happy Pencil . . ."

You, strong-limbed, noteworthy for

A brim quim, oh, vatickally

Strong! 'Atta girl! She had

A voice named Judy Brillo,

A grasp emphatic, the mosh

And moxie to quadruple th'heat

Of our dumb-adieu coupling.

Constitutive's any ritual whose antecedents

Slake a heart inconstant: I

Got brought to a nonplussable

By immurmurous perturbations, by surd.

CUSS

Cuss-drunk the Pious, you

Overwash a particular lossy comprehension

System, one whose first peck

Of notoriety is a lust-

Breath'd tango stop'd. They's no

Diviner wash for the great

Unwash'd massy fornicules than licker,

You announce, Incke of thy

Pen accrescent and dip'd. And

What perchance'd sod down thy

Brunt accrual in small-beer-

Prose? Old retainable earth, its

Malt scurve, its boreal scrum

And watery fastnesses green'd and

Blued. Besides earth and us

Leers nothing, nothing, nothing, nothing.

DIFFUSE

Diffuse with boyish grandiosity, you

Imp up a rhyme by

Flummoxing, half fire, half screed.

In Comedy, y'r little Selves

You meet, spliff city shakedown

In frail style, *poco rimbomba*

With lazy fury: the zephyr's

Back brimming with good weather.

As a voice of flowers

Ice-tines the *fortissimo* of

That singer, so divinity is

Unveil'd in psittacine bark and

Chatter. You cracker. You Polly.

Yon harangue is a right

Fell industry, and bland happiness

Batters at a severed tongue.

EMPHATIC

Emphatic's the rasp of I

In the star-eyed crosshairs

Of my cant and holy

Gibberish, zinnia'd out to th'azimuth

Where th'empty disjointure between *being*

And *meaning,* that inconquerable lag

Pettiness betwixt fallow hope &

Torn arrival's what I will

Call *God.* O such thin

Narrative'll ruin the illimitable name!

So the hectic of a

Madness's fury. The trencher'd bread

Goeth blacke as incke. I

Say set simpering criminal fires

To the 'carking anxious houses'

Of the fuggin' ambitious yessers!

FECKTHIEF

Feckthief! Sad ham-head, you

Double *usurper* who addeth none

But Sawdust to the Commonweal.

We *know* Stock in oil

(Pronounced 'awl') *lies* behind 'Shock

And Awe.' We *know* th'aw-

Shucksiness hides a murderous impenitent

Heart. We know *you,* atavistic

Gouger son of th'*original* Cheat

And retreat. We *know* that

Vaunting recklessness to commandeer *anything*

That drips Black. We know

Blood drips black. You irrecoverable

Sap of the state, you

Hazard, you God-slick'd bastard:

We know and say *no.*

GAP

Gap-tooth'd and blue, I

Dive the slurry stretches of

Sky, sky myself and goatish.

I want a minstrelsy wench.

I want a slender Russian

Apple-picker to chuck green

Granny Smiths at me, beginning

With a *zhili byli,* one

Way to momentarily lock up

A sizeable piece of continuum.

Or snatch the booger'd Starres

Downe and pluck a handy

Something, something like a muddy

Drench of ale, wise-making

And tragickal-like. Inestimable my

Pudeurs in th'amorous repudiate dark.

HOMING

Homing, shunt'd, impolitic, fox'd, I

Am the 'fyerse and skyttyssh

Hors that cast of hys

Mayster.' I am a little

World furnitured by terse and

Anarckickal argument, put it in

Gallypots. I am no more

'N a pottle of thin

Ale, howbeit a 'foles angre

Be so oft-comberus and

Malign'd, hop o' the memory'd

Wode?' I gape in vayne

Lokynge for the sylkyn shyft

Hung up on goldyn nylles

X, Y, Z: make stew

Therewith and drink abashedly thereof.

IDJIT

Idjit yclept, too well I

Noosed it, foolish and aloof:

My heart is took, my

Rubber tied. It is why

I run to bullfrog pond,

Slung in the hyssop'd dusk,

Pluck'd up in the jug-

O'-rums. Luck comes in

A dog's body and discourse

Is froth. In the jot

And tittle of Cannibal Alice's

Frantic husbandry, the world's Lithargie

So farre is groan it

Is benummed wholly. In a

Pollen air of the cutthroat

Sun, th'inexpressible exists nowhere not.

JAUNTY

Jaunty with laddish permissables, you

Point a tiny Nikon at

Corot's puttanesca-queynted efflorescence drew

Big for some wealthy turd.

It's call'd something like *Tom*

Venerus and is variably translated

"Venus with an Itch," or

"The Grassy Tumulus." Whatever that

Is in other Languages, who

Knows? You got a horrifying

Torture book open in front

Of you and you think

Maybe some goddamn General or

Other could use it for

'Image stabilization' or something, be

A big Grammarian about it.

KNOB'D

Knob'd, swell'd, and tumescing, I

Reach for th'insessorial itch. I

Consider form as an imp

Position, a means to regulate

A hole wherein we see

Our deaden'd selves with a

Scribble of not-so-indifferent

Light in our eyes. How

Big need be the story

Of our knots and libels,

Our avid manners polished-out,

Our 'foetidas and gooes'? How

Big need be our sound

Before bespoken be its name.

In the sweet commonwealth of

Little bees, not so big.

LOUD

Loud's my hangdog sonata, I

Pee roilingly into th'ebon bowl,

Night foaming up a translunary

Crescendo against whatever be feeble,

Be duff'd. Earth's an erratic,

A boulder-drop'd crumb out

The glacier's maw. Milky Way

Extended a pedicle and fill'd

It with itself the way

A paramecium moves, as if

To say it never met

A *ne plus ultra* it

Didn't like. —*So's your old*

Man. My crabbèd signature nebulaic

Trailing off into semantic froth

Looks like spit on water.

MANNER'D

Manner'd as the pipsissewa, I

'S about to squander quandary

For big score. 'Soddainly' begirt

Glam assumption tugs a tumpline

Against the buggrist habhominabull I,

That I that is but

Fucate pretence to Saint Shippe,

All menstrum and alkahest. I

Is down in the most

Vanilla interface, pdf-chunking leverageables,

Too late a stirrer, too

Late a begetter to dissolve

Th'infectious rust of innovation, yeah.

I and I we be

Bitter boys, we dodge invariable

Cheerfulness, nap on Penniless Bench.

NO

No inevitable bedder bold, you

Enter Missus Easy only in

Sir Ralph's cloathes, peg with

Her, or daub her with

A puddle. Li'l Guilt-Head

Is your monicker, obscenely uncourageous.

You fiat and deedeth by

Degrees, travelin' downwards her length

To one Great Metropolitan Toe.

Oh you can gleek up-

On occasion, cyborg to a

Myth of th'unlookt-for aloof.

Your sighs grind stars down

To points, to fire burning

Only itself, like a mind

That exists only by thinking.

ONE

One means is th'incoherent, you

Like the way it is

Having its big fat say,

Crucial, disastrous, and unrebuked. You

Like its deep & lyricke

Wayes, its habit of keeping

Time, that jolly yonker, off

Balance with its 'Farewell, slug,

Thou art in another element,'

With its lay unconsecrate drives

And choruses. Oh come ahoy

You dear 'moyst and Cloud-

Compacted braine' epic and recoiling,

Come lap at what's spilt

In the cleft, mesmerizer, come

Mug the art, rapt, eating.

PEOPLED

Peopled with unimaginable shapes, you

Draught a rough prospeckt whilst

A certain verecundinous opacity graceth

Your worship of sow-bugs,

Saps and garlands, the sopps

And frequencies of th'unshorn I.

'He unsat the unit "I"'—

Charles Olson in a fit

De-complacency re: Keats, he of

The blew presumptuous wings, lording.

So love's length grows naughty

By degrees. In our greasy

Torpor is Sum smal accrwment.

Or in pranking oneself up

To say 'No musick with-

Out discord.' *Y'r ob'd'n't, &c*

QUININE

Quinine-cinch'd and sullen, I

Infuse the periphery, I pile

Digression on digression, variegated and

Mosaickal, I make an impalpable

Art, a textured derive, a drift.

I take custody and nod,

I make obeyable th'laughter of

A disobedient sour excursus, I

Distend the coterie, belly up

To intimacy's Name drop't with

A gutta-percha'd bounce. I

Spike the period-style Ostentatory

Right down to nub &

Beck of it, I haruspicate

God-clumsy—striding the high

Balcony, eyeing the rhubarb below.

RAW

Raw, inconceivable and tetch'd, I

Feed time its own rhythms

Cook'd down to palatable mush.

Art becomes moral only by

Concealing its implacable maker's consumable

Grief in a rage of

Control, any sonnet sounding itself

To make itself, and all

Else vestigial, gaunt, left behind.

Against analysis the distilling, against

History the grudge of language:

Unreadable grass of lawns, cold

Rivers, the querulous curse of

The unfaith'd marriage of word

To bird, and rocks lit

Up by a ravaging sun.

SKINNY

Skinny-buck'd and blithe, I

Am nor soldiery, nor rank'd,

Nor Generalissimo, nor knapsack Boy.

—*That detainee got a lot*

On it plate, my word.

The way it upbraid any

Coalition of meaning: 'on corse

Of huemean events it come

Neesary for the ouilting child

On the run to bearst

Out Cabbin in the woods.'

Skeert, I am no lyrical

Diary, toss'd back by manes

Of hair and lips pursing

'No.' Art, take custody of

My mayhem, foul my breeze.

TOSS'D

Toss'd into Scotland where you

Call'd loss a season &

Scuttled the infeft, pettifoggeries of

The squelch'd heart in dolorous

Mode saw the pure urine-

Hued sun down into hardwoods,

Patching up the greenery. There

Follow'd more logical patter: stirrup

Creak and crickets scissoring at

The night. Blake: 'he who

Generalizes is an idiot.' So

Swarms of variants feed on

The wrecked text. It, too,

Proves too little, just another

Futile name sung out in

Lieu of its opus number.

UPSTIRRING

Upstirring, I comply, nuzzle I

Thy pliancy, sniff I vague

Dawns of th'anticke world. I

Am begirt with sound's brief

Indeterminate 'aye,' the sound of

Regret that perishes without memory

To mesh and well unheedy

Its mongrel draught and morsel,

Its rance tumesce and spit.

Stiff stands the solo rose

Thorn, what optics judge unmeet

To deny that I: weighing

The whole swirling promiscuous commixtion

Against th'enfeebled modern style of

I who writes 'Som heuenly

Wit doth dispone thy moveables.'

VOLCANIC

Volcanic against the fugg, you

Offer yourself up, a palpable

Orange in a flux of

Whiches. *Nomina sint numina,* oh

You shimmering monkey! Fidelity to

A discourse bangs up against

Fatuity—you cannot be th'eponymous

Hero if the novel's unnamed.

I'll call you *Lud* of

The estuaries and harborage, I'll

Call you *Dapple* in confluity,

Yours, Etc. in the scriptorium.

Here in the village of

Ystpytty Ystwyth—*Yellow'd Robes of*

The Sun. Heap up found

Things all around our wound.

WHEREAS

Whereas in 'excess Ryot, you

Hoord Corn' a drearish Year

Indeed. Down the road 'Bloomer

Bob's Hardy Mums' smudges in

Buttery light under a 'White

Cross Where the Devill hath

Dawb'd up the dirt.' 'Wasp,'

You rasp. So alloy'd is

The present to the past,

Rusts oil'd a century preceding

Proceed with damp gratitude. You

Like to commit th'impieties, bold

In simple recrudescence ho. So:

Whereas inadequate proses harry our

Nights, whereas the 'backyard makeover'

Is done: Let us sin.

XYLOGRAPHIC

Xylographic-struck kisses for you,

Poorly print'd in crabbedly-carvèd

Oak: 'Now goth sonne under

Wode.' And now 'Down on

It like a Pawnee . . . foams

The yellow-jacket Missouri.' Melville.

O the wanton burthen of

Being thy shaft in need

Of fletching, thy tyre in

Need of blowout, thy rustickal

Oaf sans-souci, thy baleen

Unflensed and incautious in bedding's

Mute moan who moil'd in

A folly 'and joy'd you

In the sack.' The taverner

Skimpeth to consolidate a quart.

YAK

Yak-rammish, stinking, thorough, you

Is a mean prey for

A bird of my pounces,

A biro at the ready,

Dirt wip't off the foolish

Moiety of me. 'Blub-cheek't,

I'de rather see a Wren

Hawke at a flye' than

Carry on so uncompelled and

Ravening. Unfinal purity indubitably haunts

All desire, don't it? Nay,

Cocky. Imperishable be the persiflage

In the ludibry, it's th'end

Impurity that valves the blow-

Outs seamlessness in the world

Makes necessary. And never suffices.

ZOOT

Zoot up tempo toss't, I

Tempest in stuck fury, against

God His supine carelessness, His

Bromides and His sweat, His

Impersonal performative Grunts. He is

A God so farre unlike

Any Bookes Knowledge, sap't He

Is. Strung out in that

Resiliency, that Redundancy, He

The God-*taint,* a compost

Like you, *Ye* to whom

I turn to turn the

Tangle straight, *Ye* for whom

The love-trumpet doth blow

To wangle up a Finishing

Touch't by courteous quotidian Snares.

V

Tears green the cheek with bright dews
                                pouring down;
Who mourns apart, alone
Oncoming swiftness in o'erlowering fate
To show what wreck is nested in deceit.

—*Ezra Pound*

ASH AND MNEMONIC

Ash-radickall'd be the asters,

Root'd in the star-kemb'd

Night, glints of divinity up

Against the bad bounce of

The brain ball, its cycloramic

Dints of genuine lustre too

Weak and silly to confute

Or stop. It's morning now,

And the night ken'd nigh

Nothing, 'a wandrynge beastely lyfe

Goone in a dramms myster

Unto playne madnes and follye.'

The sun hath a wondrous

Firk and pull, doth uncover

The sky, for whom one

Mnemonic is 'fayre mayden naked.'

BOTCH AND RETICENCE

Another day solo, leaning against

The window, no chance in

Reverie to 'botch words *Up.*'

I is just another jerk

Of Invention, a mongrel yipping

In Yellow tragicomic light. Grosseteste

Claim'd 'Light is corporeity Itself'—

And th'obscene courageous air slips

Into air, wet with impatience.

The erring mind contains no

Error incontinent, accedes not to

Labor its declivity, nor Reticence

Its many-Fortress'd Whats. Its

Vexers dance lambent over fish-

Lather'd and ungovernable seas. Mind-

Toilers to God, bidding adieu.

COLD AND ARCH

A Rebell it mought be,

And lookit that silver Sun,

A Cold cumbrous column, it

Go down like a shoe

Into mud. Regret is a

Seam in the day, bunch'd

Up surly, a mugging Cross

Alignment and gerrymander. A Plight

Wroth-scumbled and sky-scalded.

Skullduggery and scambling, Rift in

The pitkin, liturgical Spitting in

Unsanctifiable Dirt. Fear not my

Little fleck and haemorrhage, fear

Not my gospell Squall, my

Arch and holler, my sacerdotal

Imperium, my squawk, my Gun.

DAHLIAS AND STUFF

Next to mulching the dahlias

Reading the funnies with you

Tops off my dearest 'toys

Of the dumb moment' list.

Choosing flexible doings over built-

Up essentials, I got thievery-

Dibs on a sumptuous line

By Jimmy Schuyler that goes:

'Maybe I will take Vera

Vera for my stage name.'

See how I did that,

And got it to fit.

How one does it is

The stuff of legend: dalliance

Mistook for defiance, desire for

Art: its clumping veracity rued.

END AND TOOL

To no end the tongue—

Smallest member—in fiery kittle

And rash mettle gets into

A shindy with th'authorities over

A simple beatitude like filling

In the empty blanks of

A form that's marked content-

Provider. There there. It's just

More of th'essential gratuitousness that

Makes art Art, clown with

A lash to tool around

In the haecceity with. Oh

Art so pitiable in its

Ordinary units, so indubitably *motz*

And undeniably *son*. Son, that

Is, to no father known.

FRACAS AND QUILL

To pierce the savage incoherence

The apt penetralia of the

World succumb to number—two

Birds stark on a clothesline

Against a wash of sky.

Breeze and trill, or quill

And gall, the long sequacious

Notes of pitiless want hark

Back to varlet, or tinker.

In the mizzling chafe of

Day, ennui noodles its pull

Of wherewithal and albeit. Geometric

Traceries of the gone fracas—

Villon and Bertillon, yobbish grifters

Under a fierce lash—where

Hard-headedness is a testament.

GAP AND ERASURE

The lumbering bumblebee is out

Buttering up its bronze thighs

With pollen'd orbs of echinacea.

It's a period piece, a

Gap in the goldenrod, dud

Erasure against vetch-trifled embankments,

Hap what hap might. Toot

A coup I got 'promptitude

O' the toong' and I

'Misewell' make something of it.

Madder 'n a mad hen

Is how I been lately—

One summery day a redhead

Hopped off a blue bicycle,

Order'd a scoop of mocha-

Chip. Her razor smile. Period.

HA-HA AND CUT

Lying figure 'equals' *dementia.* And

Digging a new ha-ha 'is'

To replace the old posy-

Encrusted trellis. Wilmot: —*Poetry is*

An asinine name. Oh. There's

'Jemmy' Madison all in furbelows,

Hardly bigger'n *a piece of*

Soap, and what chimes out

Is vestment, an inhuman light.

Duality scrubs out a honey'd

Mouth ditty, pert particular gone

Asunder: drug-out composure. There's

Tyrone at the gym: —*Thow*

'Way the weights, a body

Got to lift it own

Body. Makes a nicer cut.

INTEGUMENT AND PILL

'I susteyne th'illusory I by

Moving I the real around.'

O me. O hyberbole, I

Fling down my blast'd spear.

I connive to slip out

Of my integument, to divulge

The vulgate bulge of my

Uncommon vulva, briefly and compliantly.

I am nothing, a whole

Barn collapsed around a pill

Bug. The British say 'wood

Louse.' I have no desire

To trouble the new orthodoxy

With such truck, affable Nullity

In socks. Behoover, our sex

Is th'embodiment of our discrepancy.

JUMBLE AND BALM

Bluster-writ is the copulatif,

Lykewyse is the place of

It, the chutney-colored rose.

A border of such dyctions

Demaundes no other ymages. It's

A lovely instant, a Jumble

Of you in cinquefeuille or

Fringed gentian, a genital cushion.

So the word *my* is

Either insolence or grace note.

And Bee-balm tosses its

Shaggy heads against sun-slopes

Abuzz with hummingbirds rigging up

Mizzenmast'n for a Schooner, one

Tall yellow Bladderwort nodding bracingly

Of 'theen fowle sclaundrous toungue.'

KUDOS AND XYSTER

Clatter in the dailies is

All box-score debt load,

Kudos to the Weimaraner, noogies

To the wisenheimer, all stalked

By the back-lit escutcheon

Of th'undiplomatickal eye. Don't call

Me Linnaeus, who never left

Uppsala, who claimed the swallow

Winter'd under water. I am

Not fond of *Liars*. Armed

With a xyster to debone

The keister of one *Criminal*

Secretary who downs *Rum*s in

The *Field*. He shalt not

Have *nothing* good chepe, he

Shalt *never* have my boy.

LANDSKIP AND FIT

Which confer'd such high additament

To my discomfort. Whose lines

Raketh. Which—like *Eben. Scritchsoule*

Poked by a sticke—is

Love's lewd Pilott. Whose restlessenesse

Abrades sinnews of landskip to

Right the commodious junk of

Man's complacency in a fit.

Whose naughty money is what

I got, & empty pocks.

Whose time uncomb'd consumes ticks

And tacks like a guinea

Hen, and songs with confidence

The bones of memory stuff'd

Into small urns. Whose antecedents

Shape a wreck'd constant heart.

MASTER AND HAZARD

Oh to stay the secondhand

Quaver with 'a pricke whiche

Dare not avovve' its name!

In the big tillage and

Husbandry of souls, one sadd

One slips, falls past the

Master of the Quire &

Quoin, tongue-embridled, and uninspectable.

Oh, blunt speech, come to

Me in your green greatcoat!

Crossed knives, chirp the kitchen

Loud! Plot-perfect, a June

Bug bangs the screen door,

Shut-out to a shut-

In. I fly my perplexity

Tether'd, hazard to pettifoggery, joss.

NEED AND ITCH

To suck Divinity, a blurriness

Struck (amongst Winch and saw-

Blade, rust-raddled in wilderness)

By Angels, by the random

Big smear. To rub up

A Drowsie sacral need, that

(Out of straggly four-tree

Orchards gone to gluttony &

Blackbirds) forces th'*inoppugnable* hand of

Renewal and itch, ungainsayably. To

Bevel-gear th'obvious with th'inflict'd.

To glew faste thy affections

To th'earth, in indisputable world-

Mindednesse. To honor thy coffer

Like unto an universal and

Publick Manuscript, no hucksterish Caprice.

OAR AND YTTERBIUM

Dost thine 'Tongue on perpetuall

Sleights and fallacies dwell,' and

Oar the air? A thrill

It is, inconsequential, irreverent, adamant

And swift. A sidelong kind

Of apery, as if th'adding

Of itch and valiant'd up

The choice, unskew the rarefaction,

And make booty of what-

Ever the language grants. Flattery,

I quairell not with *Her.*

Like ytterbium, I am clogg'd—

Not with lazie durst nots,

Nor valency's weakest crude Dusts—

But with a word's fullest

Plangency where the least domineers.

PLAIN AND UNLIKELY

Cloud-gauze nictitates the lunar

Eye, a cleansing us hide-

Bound 'churles doe heere belowe

Grutch.' Us dirty rambuncts of

The gilt heart. Two things

Hid plain: clod and cloud.

Like a credulous asse bedeck'd

In cerulean blue, I cannot

Decide if against th'evasive simile

My hard-won hard-on's

Any winsome kind of fun-

Gible code. I mean goad.

Since any sweet 'idea' is

Unlikely to order up th'whopping

Infringements, speed is essential, that

Rued boy with Mercurochromed tits.

QUIETIST AND VITALIST

Bukka White say—'That song's

Owed as water.' *Old* is

What he means—stock elliptic,

Box'd vitalist voicegram. Acute musical

Incongruity washes in to over-

Plus the computation, and tongue-

Combats assent to argufie: word-

Lawless love in feral rooms.

Ma formalist *est morte,* my

Boogie's none too good. What

Draft hath took my quietist

Nook? Tannin'd rainwater, gall'd leaf,

Mark of prong'd hoof. My

Dovecote: unimpeachable appetite for you

Still. Edward Dahlberg: 'I loathe

Any door that is open.'

RASP AND DUTY

Drub bastinadoes in the zinnias,

Fervent accountancy's again in hock.

The 'Tonus contrarius' I got

Screw'd into memory's a Rasp

Emphatic, history broken in halves.

I ai-yi-yi'd 'whence

Fyrst yr eie I eied'

Dumbstruck in the summer of

Mingus, white light'd millions binding

Heaven to earth, a burning

Whoosh cupped in hands of

Noise. Love only Nature and

Limits Terrestrial, all love's duty

Is 'Besmear'd with sluttish Time.'

Render all the malodorous *poots*

Of charwomen, there's music there.

SLIPPERY AND WRIT

Not 'the thesis of the

Plentifullest John' by Wallace Stevens,

My hiking in fleabaned flats

Of seiche-shrunk tributaries to

A lake long with light

And slippery, seeking *vestigiae*

Dei, pawprints of the Gods.

And finding 'thine Eie is

Cloid with its seeing,' finding

'Spite of thy hap, hap

Hath wel hapt' and what

Exhausts is complicity, that tandem

Of what is writ blank,

Summery, and furious, writ in

A Beam of Sunne by

The finger of God himself.

TUMULTUARY AND NOUGHT

No joynture but the hugg

Rurale, the right writ Flat-

Man, the mathematickal so-so.

—Is not. —Is so, yaaaaah,

Boo sucks to you. Such

Is my screed to my

God unjust. John Clare: 'that

That in the Act of

Seizing shrinks to nought.' Bastinado'd

By a mad crew, sniff-

Steady in this tumultuary, I

Relapse into the ordinary: juncos

Spurt off into undergrowth, flashing

White outer rectrices. Hawk plummets

Into scrub. Th'heavenly geometry squares

Up empty, like a suitcase.

UNCIAL AND ZIP

'A minute spent in sport'

Is all that gets remember'd

Of that summer. That &

'Mobbed by crows,' as if

A fourth-century Athenian with

A handsome uncial script'd rolled

Off the meagre foundational block

Of's sanity and come up

Submerged in ink. An adhesive

Light taped the galaxial whorls

To the heavens, and expired.

In the stink and boisterousness

Of a war made for

The spectacle of killing (read:

To make a killing), we

Got zip. Minus a minute.

VENOM AND OFFICE

—That ol' Daddy Deity's got

No friggin' venom on me.

The way dawn colors dawn

Up, such is contrariety drawn,

Effervescences of naught. (My opprobrious

Member delighteth so in stirring

To combat, or to combust.)

In a world where every

Part knows its proper office,

(Or orifice) and all Corrumptions

Get produced by Motions Irregular,

Stinking Foggs, Moisturous Parts, I

Add yellow orpiments to sad-

Assed smutt, and rise ardent

To a coming near 'a

Clout'd innocencie,' nigh a *rapprochement*.

WAR AND JERK

You, yond thing, one of

The 'sowdgers that fyghte' whilst

Us 'Civill swaines groe savedge,

Rude, and wilde,' for that

Is what a foreign war

Bringeth, not more struttle (fish),

Nor pooties (snails), nor goods

To rattle th'unhusbanded sad nation.

And *you,* fucker, Texas pecker-

Wood: more moral a clod

Of sun-blast'd earth is,

More credulous an Asse hauling

A cloud behind. If only

That Asse'd chose you, smirker,

Jug-ear'd contemptuous jerk, to

Haul off into the burn.

XENON AND KIN

Autumn unrolls its monotonous lawn

Languor, its stranglehold fidelity to

A Discourse of pied type

And confinement recommends a winter

Contentment of whey, asses milk,

Spawnwater. Like xenon—colorless, inert,

Gaseous—that white season like

A universell publik Manuscript expans'd

To the eyes of all.

Spring in saddrest hils is

A sparrowhawk's choppy wing-work

To hang in place. Summer's

White-faced heifers: plodding red

Ruminant things. A black boy's

Rural kin cain't get to

No capital for no funeral.

YES AND GAG

Tuft'd buff cattails lit by

Sunup, Nat Adderley blowing cornet.

Ammo on the dash of

Every truck I pass. —*Yes,*

Ma'am, that was a plywood

Chapel doghouse. —*No, ma'am, it*

Wudn't no gag funeral parlor.

In 'the general scramble &

Pant' of upright industry, it

Is a picture of John

Clare making a pawky embouchure

To draw out the choric

Woodsnipe that keeps me vertical,

And effectually hamstrings any pretence

My hoyden'd counterblast to objectivist

Stringency's got. Listen to it.

ZIGGURAT AND LURCH

'I like to pull a

Melody slow, pull it all

The way here to Hatch-

A-Pea.' Some bandleader or

Other. The point is cadence

And event, the grease pencil

Jabbing the renegade brow of

The clown. So the Fokker

Trailing manufactured smoke built up

A ziggurat over th'arts quad.

So the lurch and ratio

Of a made thing's making.

Rose and fanny obstacle-course

And my duped vogue for

Horseplay'll add naught but saw-

Dust to the common weal.

Acknowledgments

Some of these poems originally appeared in the following publications: *1913: A Magazine of Forms, American Letters & Commentary, Backwards City Review, Bird Dog, Boston Review, The Brooklyn Rail, Cello Entry, Chicago Review, Columbia Poetry Review, Conundrum, Critical Quarterly, Crowd, Damn the Caesars, Electronic Poetry Review, Epoch, Famous Reporter, Fence, Free Verse, Gam, Good Foot, Harper's, Intercapillary Space, Jacket, LIT, Magazine Cypress, The Modern Review, Near South, New American Writing, The New Review of Literature, No: A Journal of the Arts, Notre Dame Review, Origin, Parakeet, Poetry Review, The Poker, Puppy Flowers, Rossocorpolingua, Skald, Sonora Review, Typo, Vanitas, Verse, Where We Put Our Hats, Xantippe,* and *Your Black Eye.*

My thanks to all the editors, publishers, readers and interlocutors. Particular thanks, too, to Gianluca Rizzo, who translated four poems for *Rossocorpolingua* into Italian, to Mark Scroggins, who generously wrote the introduction, with both readerly aplomb and writerly verve, and to Luigi Ballerini, who caught my mid-Zoom-reading mutter about an unpublished manuscript and promptly asked to see it.

Books published by Agincourt Press in the Opuntia Series

Gianfranco Contini, *An Idea of Dante* (2021)
Giani Stuparich, *One Year of School and The Island* (2021)
Michela Dall'Aglio, *In the Beginning There Was Freedom. An Itinerary between Science, Philosophy, and Faith* (2020)
Mariano Bàino, *Yellow Fax and Other Poems* (2019)
Alfredo Giuliani (ed.), *I Novissimi* (2017)
Gianluca Rizzo (ed.), *On the Fringe of the Neoavantgarde / Ai confine della neoavanguardia, Palermo 1963 – Los Angeles 2013* (2017)
Massimo Ciavolella and Gianluca Rizzo (ed.), *Savage Words: Invectives as a Literary Genre* (2016)
Massimo Ciavolella and Gianluca Rizzo (ed.), *Like Doves Summoned by Desire: Dante's New Life in 20th Century Literature and Cinema. Essays in memory of Amilcare Iannucci* (2012)
Elio Pagliarani, *The Girl Carla and Other Poems* (2009) Maurizio Cucchi, *The Missing* (2008)
Remo Bodei, *We, The Divided: Ethos, Politics, and Culture in Post-War Italy, 1943-2006* (2006)
Standard Shaefer, *Water & Power* (2005)
Robert Crosson, *The Day Sam Goldwyn Stepped off the Train* (2004)
Paul Vangelisti, *Embarrassment of Survival* (2001)

www.ingramcontent.com/pod-product-compliance
Lightning Source LLC
Chambersburg PA
CBHW030152100526
44592CB00009B/247